Why Therapy? Why Not.

ALTHILIA MOORE

Why Therapy? Why Not.

The Nots ...

There are numerous reasons why therapy has its challenges. There are many people who experience the lesser in the therapy room and have no sense of acceptance from the individual representing acceptance.

The clinician asking to hear about their experience just to take this information to judge it with their opinion. This person says blatantly "I understand," but does not look like their own typing and has no real understanding of the truths of this person's experience.

Judgement is not acceptable in the therapy environment, but when it happens this should be the time to search for a therapist who is a better match. Remember, therapy is for you. Period.

I know Behavioral Therapy Service has its downfalls with different groups and populations of people and more over marginalized people. Which makes it difficult for those to continue their pursuit to change. Marginalized groups are often left feeling hopeless about their situations. They need their affordable living, education, healthcare, housing, and family support in general.

It is difficult to feel comfortable and to consider what your everyday experience is in America while being reminded every day that you are different, as if being different is a crime or a bad thing. The corporate lies that have trailed the paths in our covert policies for decades have run its course, and the truth be told about the racism in America.

We have all had experience with the wars of racism in America, both past, present in so many different forms. The latest de facto with the attack on the Capitol of the U.S. from domestic terrorists, who believe they have lost their freedom, who prove to have any respect to difference and rights in the democracy of fair voting practices in America.

I consider myself a beautiful black woman, whose parents and grandparents were proud African American women and men. Some served in the U.S. military and some provided service to others in need on a day-to-day basis. The women before me, my ancestors, were brought here against their will. No matter who made the trade, it was made, and that makes this land and country ours too.

This land has contributed to those whose ancestors contributed to it first, and especially for those who were not compensated for their free, hard labor. I give homage to them first. This is what blood, sweat, and tears are in the eye of sacrifice and commitment.

My ancestors were important enough to feed their white masters, clean their clothes, breastfeed their babies, and so much more. But that was not enough to get a thank you or fair compensation for their hard work. This is my past, and I suggest you do your own work and find out more about you when you are able, because there is where your true strength lies.

This is not for you if you can't handle the truth. I am not the person who wants to talk about other people's comfort with privilege. While some glean in the faces of others as though they are sorry for the disastrous behavior blacks have lived with in America and supposedly "out of the know."

I would be embarrassed to say I have privilege and that has shortchanged your ability. But there are those who flaunt this personality as though they seek this weak praise. This arrogance is less important, and only serves to assure me of my true worth, which has been wanted by many.

Demand your respect and to be served in human services built for yourselves. You have rights, both as a citizen and as a human that need to be practiced in your day-to-day struggles. Sometimes these gatekeepers act like you are asking her for money out of her own pocket. Do not allow the attitude of the person whose job is to service your paperwork be the determinant of your receiving what initially is yours, your human services.

Allow this person to read in between the lines of "Giving up is not an option" and sign your consent forms. This is your consent to serve you, and you deserve service from a country that owes you respect because you are a human being. Your wellbeing is all that is important, whether they like it or not. It is not your problem at all.

The fake, soft stories around the history told to us from day one has been the ugliest truth about America and the soft ground it has been living on. It is the arrogance of others who think this way and have seats in the public office who should have never been there and should not be there today.

These individuals are not service people or community driven, rather they are criminal minded, divisive, and hurtful to the free world that is deserved by every human life. Social issues affect mental health in the worst way and open the gateway for individuals to decompensate with regard to how they function on a day-to-day basis.

How does a person live with poor housing, high-crime neighborhoods, poor-quality food, and poor education and then expect to go into society with a happy dance and a treat-others-like-you-want-to-be-treated attitude?

Yes. The way it sounds is the way it feels for those who are marginalized on a generational-by-generation basis, when you are in need and desperate for your daily necessities and then rejected anywhere from the doctor's office, to the Welfare line, to the bank and when requesting a loan. No has become a familiar word that is now the first expectation of the service world.

At a minimum, can there be a sense of safety in the therapy room? I don't have a sense of safety in my home because ... in my family because ... in my school because ... a trusted friend because .... Can I please have a sense of safety in my therapy room? Yes. You can.

Why? Because this established relationship comes with boundaries.

When boundaries are crossed, the relationship must end. In some cases, this is a first-time relationship for those who can initially grow outside of the therapy room and on to their other, established relationships.

This is called a person-centered approach, a therapy approach that I use a lot that was first introduced by Carl Rogers. When I work with clients, it is important to me that they have a good understanding of who I am. I am transparent in a way that helps them feel safe and heard. This part of my orientation is most important because of the sense of community it establishes, and that I hope to see change for the better.

I work with clients who are in need. Not only the client who can afford therapy, but the one who cannot afford it as well, I hold an empathy for all walks of life.

What is the financial situation for the working taxpayer? Or, better yet, a blue-collar worker who is not able to purchase or afford insurance coverage to receive behavioral services. Or even better, for someone who receives social services and gets a state healthcare plan only to find out the plan does not include behavioral health services.

When politicians and governments continue down a path that deny services to those who are in need and deserve them the most, it continues to support poor leadership across from those responsible and lack of regard for the people involved.

These situations are up for grabs with voting and self-advocating. Each day I am hopeful and believe that a healthier America is coming. With new leadership in place, I am hopeful for some of these dynamics to have radical change in the systems of America to work for all Americans.

The Stigma...

Adults who are in their fifties or older can provide some very interesting reasons why therapy is nothing but a waste of time. This is a no-changing game for anyone, but when you enter the therapy room for yourself you rarely want to leave. That is an interesting phenomenon from those who seek to downplay therapy and have never entered the environment.

I recommend giving it a try and then share your experience, whether good or bad. All reviews are helpful to the improvement process, particularly for those who suggest that therapy cannot work and who understand that their current solution has not helped and continues to not help them and for those who are afraid to talk to someone they do not know well.

This is especially for you! Those around you have failed you in the listening arena, whether they just do not understand or if they are unwilling to stretch their olive branch. None of it helps you in your most-needed areas. This now becomes more of a burden for you to carry feelings that are even more hurtful. For those of you who have difficulty with change and accepting change, this is for you, too.

I think this is a bonus to you, especially when life says you are not able to change your behaviors, choices, and views. You prove to enjoy life in a way that is inspirational to those who look up to you. While these are examples of why therapy is a difficult task for those with different backgrounds, they are valid reasons why it is a helpful task to take on for one's self care.

Why Yes?

Because, on average, your problem or struggle is not yours alone. This does not speak to how it feels for those who are lonely and isolated. This is true about the devastation of isolation. Americans are isolated with the issues it is not willing to face head on and change. Your problems, your struggles, are America's problems and struggles. Period.

Americans are responsible for one another, and because this is not preached beginning in the home or school system, it is misunderstood throughout life. You matter…

Why?

If you are experiencing grief, discrimination, loneliness, or isolation; feel that your life needs change; lack in family support and trusted relationships; have parenting struggles, marital conflicts, or financial hardships; or need a career or career change, then this journal book is for you! Began your search for healing and change to freedom.

The Journal Book

This journal book will help open your mind to the thoughts that may be of concern to you and have been lingering around without any resolution. This journal will guide you to the first steps to saying yes.

Yes to investing in yourself like never before. Like many others, you may invest in yourself with the clothes you wear, the car you drive, the house you live in (some), and your clean outlook on life. This outlook keeps you protected, in the sense that it keeps you isolated and disconnected from your truth.

No, I am not selling a product or offering a guarantee on a product. Rather, as a psychotherapist I am an advocate for the client and the therapist or clinician. I am on both sides of this. I am experiencing life in a freedom I never knew existed because there were some people who sat in a room with me and just listened.

They listened without judgement; offered without attitude; guided without holding back. I want you to have this too. Someone may not look like you, but every experience is an experience worth sharing with someone else. Again, self-advocating starts here.

Why?

Because taking care of your health is conducive to taking care of your brain and your mind. Your health consists of your mind, body, and soul, correct? Then why do we stop at medical health or spiritual health when all of these facilities rely on the brain's function.

There is nothing wrong with feeling free in life while living in a world of destruction and expectation. If you want more of you and more of an understanding of yourself, let us start here. Open to what challenges you and has you stuck. Let us begin here with some thoughts to consider.

Anxiety Symptoms

Anxiety symptoms vary and have different reasons why they exist. We can explain this on a one-to-one basis. If you believe you are feeling nervous, anxious, tremors, panic, or racing thoughts, to name a few, take some time and apply these steps.

- Sit down and take in a long, deep breath. Count to six, hold for two seconds, and breathe out, counting to four or five seconds.

- Sit down or lie down on a mat, close your eyes, and affirm yourself with words of kindness, love, and encouragement. Repeat this until it resonates.

- Take a walk or run

- Listen to some soft music

Depressive Mood

Depression has many facets about where and why it exists. We can explain this more closely on a one-to-one basis. More importantly, if your experiencing sadness, crying a lot, are frustrated, confused, lack in concentration, or have insomnia, just to name a few, try these tips while waiting for your appointment.

- Make a list of how long this has been going on and when it started if you can. If not, it is okay. We'll get there.

- Journal your mood, feelings, and thoughts for your professional.

- Eat healthy foods and drink plenty of fluids if possible.

- Take naps if needed.

- Take walks and exercise.

- Change clothes once or twice a day.

Vision Boards

Make a vision board. Vision boards are helpful in capturing those thoughts, desires wanting to live out and provides a space for your review. Vision boards are for individuals, couples, or the whole family together!

- Use a background of some sort, large construction paper, cardboard, laminated paper.

- Cut up magazine pictures or quotes.

- Search for affirmations or make up your own.

- Give your vision board a title

Grounding Exercises can help with Breathing and Focus.

- Count backward from five to one.

- Name five things you can see right now.

- Name four things you can feel right now.

- Name three things you smell right now.

- Name two things you can taste right now.

- Name one thing great about yourself right now

These are general tips to take prior to setting your appointment or while you are waiting for your appointment to take place. If these situations are urgent, unbearable, or persistent, please do not hesitate to contact 911 or proceed to your local hospital. You may need urgent attention. This is not diagnosing, but providing you with an insight into the therapeutic process.

Let us get started on you. Keep your therapy guidebook for your before-and-after snapshot of your journey. You can check in on yourself mid-way and when your therapy goals have been met successfully. This may be the start, but you will be the one to get to your finish line when you are able.

Let us respond to the next questions and use these questions as a guide to your new you. Your new understanding of your underlining self-concerns.

I am bothered by...

I have agony because ...

I am saddened with ...

If I had the power to change ...

My growth would start here if I had ...

I envision myself here ...

Try the Mirror Test

Stare in the mirror and see both sides of yourself. Listen to the words spoken and record them here.

My mirror test said ...

I feel this about myself when ...

I know this about myself ...

I have Hopes for ...

I am Ready and Willing to start here ...

The first thing I want to change is ...